GOD AND GOODNIGHT MOON

FINDING SPIRITUALITY IN STORYBOOKS FOR CHILDREN

Copyright © 2014 by Open Waters Publishing
All rights reserved.

Open Waters Publishing
700 Prospect Avenue
Cleveland, Ohio 44115
www.openwaterspublishing.com

Portions of this book were previously published as
*Children Learn What They Read: Seeing the Presence
of God Through Selected Storybooks*, by Carolyn Landers
Pettigrew and Dawn Karima Pettigrew, © United Church Press.

Scripture quotations taken or adapted from the
New Revised Standard Version Bible, copyright
© 1989 National Council of Churches of Christ in
the United States of America. Used by permission.
All rights reserved.

Design by Robyn Henderson Nordstrom

Printed in the United States of America

First Edition: July 2014

10 9 8 7 6 5 4 3 2 1

Open Waters Publishing is an imprint of The Pilgrim Press.
The Open Waters Publishing name and logo are trademarks
of Local Church Ministries, the United Church of Christ.

ISBN 978-0-8298-2020-1

CONTENTS

The Big Box by Toni Morrison, with Slade Morrison | 4

Brother Eagle, Sister Sky: A Message from Chief Seattle by Chief Seattle | 6

Brundibar by Tony Kushner | 8

The Crane Wife by Sumiko Yagawa | 10

Crow Boy by Taro Yashima | 12

The Gardener by Sarah Stewart | 14

God's Paintbrush by Sandy Eisenberg Sasso | 18

Goodnight Moon by Margaret Wise Brown | 20

Grandad's Prayers of the Earth by Douglas Wood | 22

Guess How Much I Love You by Sam McBratney | 24

The Hello, Goodbye Window by Norton Juster | 26

Hope by Isabell Monk | 28

In God's Name by Sandy Eisenberg Sasso | 32

Joseph Had a Little Overcoat by Simms Taback | 34

Kitten's First Full Moon by Kevin Henkes | 36

Mama, Do You Love Me? by Barbara M. Joosse | 40

Oliver Button is a Sissy by Tomie dePaola | 42

On the Day You Were Born by Debra Frasier | 44

The Patchwork Quilt by Valerie Flournoy | 46

People by Peter Spier | 48

Peter's Chair by Ezra Jack Keats | 50

The Runaway Bunny by Margaret Wise Brown | 52

The Snowy Day by Ezra Jack Keats | 54

Something Special for Me by Vera B. Williams | 56

The Story of Ruby Bridges by Robert Coles | 58

Stranger in the Woods: A Photographic Fantasy by Carl R. Sams II and Jean Stoick | 60

This is Not My Hat by Jon Klassen | 64

This Land is Your Land by Woody Guthrie | 68

The Velveteen Rabbit by Margery Williams | 70

What's Wrong with Timmy? by Maria Shriver | 72

When I Was Young in the Mountains by Cynthia Rylant | 76

Appendix I | 79

Appendix II | 81

Appendix III | 89

THE BIG BOX

BY TONI MORRISON, WITH SLADE MORRISON
ILLUSTRATED BY GISELLE POTTER

New York: Hyperion/Jump at the Sun, 1999

Synopsis:

A trio of children, representing a variety of races, are sentenced to "live in a big brown box" because they do not live by the rules imposed by teachers, neighbors, and relatives. Adults determine that the children "can't handle their freedom," even though the children assert that animals in nature are allowed to do whatever they need to do. The children do many of the things that are expected of them, yet their failures to meet adult expectations force them to live in a box. Their parents visit, bringing images of the outside world and plenty of costly gifts, yet have very little interaction with their children. This story is a social commentary on the prevalence of materialism, the deterioration of interpersonal relationships, and the meaning and use of freedom.

Spiritual themes:

family relationships, each individual is unique, obedience to parents and teachers, the dangers of substituting material things for spiritual/personal relationships (materialism), liberty rather than rebellion, decision making, personal accountability, diversity of creation and nature

Scriptural application:

Children, obey your parents in the Lord,
for this is right.—Ephesians 6:1

Now the Lord is the Spirit, and where the
Spirit of the Lord is, there is freedom.—2 Corinthians 3:17

Spiritual reflection:

1. Why do we have rules? Why are rules important? When are rules good for us? Are there any times that you don't understand the rules that your parents/guardians make for you? According to the scripture, what should you do then?

2. Why do you think that the parents brought gifts when they came to visit? Did having gifts make it any easier for the children to live in the box? Why or why not?

Activity:
Children's Box

Materials needed:

small gift/shoe boxes, magazines with photographs, water-soluble glue, scissors, markers/crayons

If you lived in a box, what would be in it? Encourage children to cut out pictures and glue them on the inside of their box. When they are finished, ask them to draw a door on the inside. Share 2 Corinthians 3:17 with them. Then, ask them to draw a door on the OUTSIDE of their box.

BROTHER EAGLE, SISTER SKY: A MESSAGE FROM CHIEF SEATTLE

BY CHIEF SEATTLE
PAINTINGS BY SUSAN JEFFERS

New York: Dial, 1991

Synopsis:

This 1992 Abby Award Winner combines a famous speech, attributed to Chief Seattle, with intricate pen ink and dye artwork. This book introduces children to genocide and displacement that relocated American Indians to reservations by describing the conditions that led Chief Seattle to make his noted speech. Jeffers illustrates Chief Seattle's concerned refusal to sell land with detailed pictures. Each picture demonstrates the chief's assertion that every animal, insect, person, and life form are connected in a "web" of life. As a result, the earth and its environment must be preserved. *Brother Eagle, Sister Sky* is a portrayal of a loving American Indian family. This book also provides a thought-provoking commentary on interdependence and the environment.

Spiritual themes:

family love, stewardship of the environment, working together, cooperation, beauty, majesty, diversity, and importance of God's creation, connection between all life forms, respect for traditions and ancestors, preservation of the environment, treating others as you would like to be treated

Scriptural application:

The earth is the Lord's and all that is in it, the world,
and those who live in it. —Psalm 24:1

Spiritual reflection:

1. In the story, a boy and his family see lots of animals, birds, insects, and other creatures around them each day. Name some of them. What kinds of animals, birds, insects, and other life do you see around you? How are they all connected to you? To each other?

2. Why do you think that God made so many different kinds of creatures? How does what people do to the earth affect these creatures? the planet? other people? themselves? How could realizing that cause us to change our behavior?

Activity:

On index cards or pieces of paper, write the names of various kinds of animals, insects, fish, birds, environmental features (air, rivers, mountains, etc.). Fold them and put them in a container. Let the child pick out two or three of them. Ask the child or each child, in turn, to tell how they think that these seemingly unrelated creatures may be related to each other and then to people/themselves. (Children may receive help from adults or other children if they need it.)

BRUNDIBAR

RETOLD BY TONY KUSHNER
ILLUSTRATED BY MAURICE SENDAK

New York: Michael DiCapua Books/Hyperion Books for Children, 2003

Synopsis:

This book is based on a Czech opera of the same name first performed in 1938. Brother and sister, Aninku and Pepicek, are sent to town to find milk for their sick mother. She needs this to become well. They discover they need money to purchase the milk and they have none. Aninku and Pepicek brainstorm ways to earn the money for the milk finally settling on singing a song in hopes people will pay them for it. Their plan is thwarted by Brundibar, a bellowing, fearsome hurdy-gurdy grinder who makes so much noise no one can hear their song. The children pretend they are bears in hopes of scaring off Brundibar. Instead, Brundibar becomes even scarier and frightens the children away. They are very sad and hide in an alley. In the alley they meet a talking sparrow and a talking cat. A talking dog joins them and the bird and animals vow to help the children beat Brundibar. The dog suggests they need to gather more children around them for help. The sparrow flies away gathering 300 school children together. The children decide to sing a song to raise money for the milk for Aninku and Pepicek's mother. The crowds love the song and throw coins into the children's milk bucket. Brundibar protests the song and runs off with the milk bucket. The animals and children chase him and he is forced to relinquish the bucket and the coins. The children are able to buy the milk for their sick mother as the bully, Brundibar, is defeated.

Spiritual themes:

the triumph of Good over Evil, the need for community to accomplish things one or two people cannot do by themselves, helping others, family relationships.

Scriptural application:

Do not be overcome by evil, but overcome evil with good.—Romans 12:21

Do not neglect to do good and to share what you have, for such sacrifices are pleasing to God.—Hebrews 13:16

Spiritual reflection:

1. Why do you think the sparrow, the cat, and the dog decided to help Aninku and Pepicek? Why did the 300 children help? Do you think it was OK for them to skip school to do this? What does the Scripture say about helping in this kind of situation?
2. Have you ever met anyone like Brundibar? What was it like? Who helped you in this situation?

Activity:
Good Deeds

Materials needed:

White paper, crayons or markers.

Pass out the drawing materials to the children. Ask them to think of a time when they did something good for someone else or a time when they helped someone. Have them draw a picture of this. When the children are finished with their drawings have them share their pictures and their meaning with the rest of the group.

THE CRANE WIFE

BY SUMIKO YAGAWA
ILLUSTRATED BY SUEKICHI AKABA
TRANSLATED BY KATHERINE PATTERSON

New York: William Morrow, 1981

Synopsis:

Yohei patiently nurses a wounded crane. A short time later, a beautiful woman comes to marry him. She uses her gifts and talents to weave special fabric for him and to reward him for his kind heart.

Spiritual themes:

helping the wounded and hurting, mercy, gentleness, giving, marriage, sharing, art, using gifts and talents

Scriptural application:

He answered, 'You shall love the Lord your God with all your heart, and with all your soul, and with all your strength, and with all your mind; and your neighbor as yourself.' And he said to him, 'You have given the right answer; do this, and you will live.' But wanting to justify himself, he asked Jesus, 'And who is my neighbor?' Jesus replied, 'A man was going down

from Jerusalem to Jericho, and fell into the hands of robbers, who stripped him, beat him, and went away, leaving him half dead. Now by chance a priest was going down that road; and when he saw him, he passed by on the other side. So likewise a Levite, when he came to the place and saw him, passed by on the other side. But a Samaritan while traveling came near him; and when he saw him, he was moved with pity. He went to him and bandaged his wounds, having poured oil and wine on them. Then he put him on his own animal, brought him to an inn, and took care of him. The next day he took out two denarii, gave them to the innkeeper, and said, 'Take care of him; and when I come back, I will repay you whatever more you spend.' Which of these three, do you think, was a neighbor to the man who fell into the hands of the robbers?' He said, 'The one who showed him mercy.' Jesus said to him, 'Go and do likewise.'
—Luke 10:27–37

Spiritual reflection:

1. In the Bible story we read, a man has compassion for another man in trouble. How does God want us to treat other people?

2. How does Yohei treat the crane in the story? What happens to him because of his kindness?

3. Do you know anyone who is hurting or who needs kindness? What can you do to help them?

Activity:
Weavings

Materials needed:

felt squares, various colors of yarn, scissors

Fold felt square in half, lengthwise. Make cuts of varying widths across the square, without cutting all the way across. Unfold the felt square. Cut pieces of yarn approximately one inch longer at each end than the felt square. Using various colors of yarn, weave the yarn through the slits, over and under the felt. Repeat until a colorful pattern is woven.

CROW BOY

BY TARO YASHIMA

New York: Viking, 1955

Synopsis:

This Caldecott Honor Book offers an opportunity for children to explore the world of those who are differently abled. A Japanese boy attends school each day, but learning is a challenge for him. The other children tease him because he does not speak to them and seems to be intellectually limited. Finally, the boy achieves some basic educational skills and shows that he has worth, value, and gifts of his own to offer others.

Spiritual themes:

kindness, tolerance, different levels of physical/mental ability, acceptance of others, giving, school dynamics, education, patience, self-control, meekness, understanding, empathy, God's love and plan for each person

Scriptural application:

Bear one another's burdens, and in this way you will fulfill the law of Christ.—Galatians 6:2

Spiritual reflection:

1. How is the boy in the story different from the other children? Why do they tease him? Why do you think that people mistreat people who do not seem to be like everyone else?

2. How does the Bible verse tell us that we are supposed to treat those who are different, or are not able to do what we can do?

3. Is there someone at your school or church that seems "different" from other people? How do people treat them? How do you treat them? How do you think that God would want you to treat them? Do you need to change the way that you treat them?

Activity:
The Beauty of Diversity

Materials needed:

paper, scissors, crayons, markers

The story portrays a boy who seems to be "different." What would the world be like if everyone was the same? Ask the children to fold the paper into an accordion fold and draw the outline of a person on it. Cut out the outline into paper dolls. When the children unfold the connected dolls, they will all look alike. Discuss how the world would be if everyone was alike. Then, ask the children to decorate each doll so that they are all different. Discuss what is better about a world where everyone is different.

THE GARDENER

BY SARAH STEWART
ILLUSTRATED BY DAVID SMALL

New York: Farrar, Straus, Giroux, 1997

Synopsis:

When Lydia Grace Finch's family is hit hard by economic depression, she travels to the city to stay with her Uncle Jim. Uncle Jim never smiles, but Lydia Grace sets out to make him a surprise that will cause him to grin from ear to ear. Lydia Grace works in Uncle Jim's bakery, where she builds friendships with Emma and Ed, African American coworkers. Lydia Grace brings seeds with her from the country, and her grandmother sends her plants and seeds. Lydia Grace keeps in touch with her family by sending detailed letters, which are the narration for the book. Soon, the bakery is covered with flowers and Lydia Grace and Emma make it a place of life and light. The customers increase (even sharing their plants with "the gardener") and Uncle Jim is happier. Finally, Lydia Grace shows Uncle Jim her great surprise—a flower garden on the roof! Uncle Jim doesn't smile, but he makes Lydia Grace a cake covered with flowers and shows his softer side as his niece prepares to leave. A Caldecott Honor Book, *The Gardener* features colorful pictures and an admirable female main character.

Spiritual themes:

sharing, love, hard work, family love and relationships, giving, generosity, acceptance of others, persistence, love for neighbors, giving even when it doesn't seem effective or appreciated, turning hardship into opportunity, overcoming adversity, affection, friendship, letter writing and communication, intergenerational friendship, mentoring, respect for nature, appreciation for home and family, contentment, resilience, willingness to work and learn

Scriptural application:

Love never ends.—1 Corinthians 13:8

Spiritual reflection:

1. The Bible says that love never ends. When Lydia Grace first gave Uncle Jim a poem, he didn't smile, yet she kept trying to do something that would make him smile. What would have happened if she had given up? What happened because she kept showing love to Uncle Jim?

2. What ways did Lydia Grace show love to Uncle Jim? Who showed love to Lydia Grace? How did Uncle Jim show love to Lydia Grace? How did Emma and Ed show their love to her? How did the neighbors show love to Lydia Grace?

3. How do you show love to the people in your life? How can you show them that you love them even more? When have you shown love to people with good results?

Activity:
Make Someone Smile

Materials needed:

various colors of tissue paper (preferably cut into squares), scissors, pipe cleaners, ribbon

Lydia Grace had plenty of room to garden in the country. When she got to the city, she didn't let that stop her. She used creativity to grow plants in window gardens and on the roof. Crush and twist squares of tissue paper into "flowers." Use pipe cleaners for stems. Make a "bouquet of flowers" and tie it together with string, or wrap it in paper. Present the bouquet to someone that you think needs to smile today.

GOD'S PAINTBRUSH

BY SANDY EISENBERG SASSO
ILLUSTRATED BY ANNETTE C. COMPTON

Woodstock, Vermont: Jewish Lights, 1992

Synopsis:

Who is God? This book encourages children to explore the wonder of God through its interactive format. Colors, joy, and multiculturalism invite children to think of God as Someone Who loves them and is a Friend to them. This book offers adults the opportunity to begin discussions about God with their children.

Spiritual themes:

God, love, multiculturalism, creation, diversity, friendship, identity, creativity, imagination, joy, praise, being thankful, families, acceptance

Scriptural application:

Now when Jesus came into the district of Caesarea Philippi, he asked his disciples, 'Who do people say that the Son of Man is?' And they said, 'Some say John the Baptist, but others Elijah, and still others Jeremiah or

one of the prophets.' He said to them, 'But who do you say that I am?' Simon Peter answered, 'You are the Messiah, the Son of the living God.' And Jesus answered him, 'Blessed are you, Simon son of Jonah! For flesh and blood has not revealed this to you, but my [Parent] in heaven.'
—Matthew 16:13–17

Spiritual reflection:
1. Who do you think God is?
2. People see God in many different ways. Why do you think that is?

Activity:
Three-Dimensional World

Materials needed:

colored tissue paper, crayons/markers, glue, construction paper

Encourage children to think about the beauty of God's creation and design. Ask them to draw the outlines of a picture that they think could be painted with "God's paintbrush." It is best to draw large shapes. Do not color them in or add detail. Next, ask the children to fill in their outlines by tearing off small pieces of colored tissue paper, scrunching them, and placing a dot of glue on the bottom. Then, place the piece within the outline of the object that it is coloring. Repeat until each outline is filled with tissue paper. The result will be a textured, three-dimensional picture.

GOODNIGHT MOON

BY MARGARET WISE BROWN
PICTURES BY CLEMENT HURD

New York: Harper, 1947

Synopsis:

A touching portrayal of a rabbit's bedtime ritual. While bidding goodnight to its surroundings, the rabbit prepares for peaceful sleep.

Spiritual theme:

peace, family love, the blessing of rest and sleep, God's creation

Scriptural application:

I lie down and sleep; I wake again,
for the Lord sustains me. —Psalm 3:5

I will both lie down and sleep in peace; for you alone,
O Lord, make me lie down in safety. —Psalm 4:8

Spiritual reflection:

1. Why do you think that God made nighttime? Why is it good for us to sleep? Do you ever wish you didn't have to go to bed? Why?

2. Have you ever been scared at night? How does naming the things in the room help the rabbit to fall asleep peacefully?

Activity:
Bedtime Prayer Reminder

Materials needed:

Popsicle sticks (widest available), glue, markers

Give each child two Popsicle sticks and a piece of string. Ask them to think about the people, things, and concerns that they want to pray about before bed each night. Have the children draw pictures that represent each or write each object of prayer on the sticks (both sides can be used). Then, glue the sticks together in the shape of a cross. Placed beside their beds, this bedtime prayer reminder can help children remember to say their prayers. The Bible verses that we read assure us that God will watch over the people of God and protect them as they sleep. Encourage the children to pray without ceasing, including each night before bedtime.

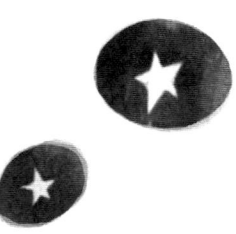

GRANDAD'S PRAYERS
OF THE EARTH

BY DOUGLAS WOOD
ILLUSTRATED BY P J. LYNCH

Cambridge, Massachusetts: Candlewick, 1999

Synopsis:

A young boy and his grandfather journey through the forests. As they walk, the boy asks his grandfather about the meaning and definition of prayer. His grandfather explains the beauty and majesty of the natural world. Further, he teaches the boy about creative, expressive prayers prayed by people in all situations, conditions, and how prayer changes the people who pray. This lesson is tested when the grandfather dies and the boy must turn to prayer for comfort and hope. Vivid watercolors depict this rural Caucasian American family's faith journey and the environment that surrounds them.

Spiritual themes:

prayer, faith, love, family love, intergenerational interaction, death, environmental awareness, grief and sorrow, hope, comfort, stewardship of the environment, beauty, diversity and value of God's creation, communication, personal relationship with God

Scriptural application:

Pray without ceasing.—1 Thessalonians 5:17

Spiritual reflection:

1. How much does the Word of God tell us we should pray? When do you pray? How does prayer make you feel? If you don't pray, why don't you?

2. The boy's grandfather told him that "people pray some of the most wonderful prayers of all." What kinds of things do you pray about? What kind of things do you say to God?

3. In the book, the boy prays after his grandfather dies. How does praying help him to deal with his loss? Did you ever lose someone or feel very sad? How could praying help/have helped you?

4. According to the book, prayer changes the people who pray. How did praying change the boy in the story? How has prayer changed you or something in your life?

Activity:
Body Prayer

Throughout the Bible, many different positions are shown for praying. King Solomon kneeled on his knees before God and spread his hands toward Heaven (2 Chronicles 6), while Daniel knelt (Daniel 6). Elijah bowed down toward the ground with his face toward the earth (1 Kings 18). King David sat before the Lord (2 Samuel 7), yet one of his Psalms says that he thought about God while resting in bed (Psalm 4). The grandfather in the story says that many of the things that we do are forms of prayers. Standing and singing (Psalm 135), playing instruments and dancing (Psalm 150), shouting (Psalm 132), and lifting holy hands (1 Timothy 2) are some of the positions that the Bible shows us for prayer. Encourage the children to use these positions in a time of body prayer. Then, have them share other things that they do that God could consider acts of worship.

GUESS HOW MUCH I LOVE YOU

BY SAM MCBRATNEY
ILLUSTRATED BY ANITA JERAM

Cambridge, Massachusetts: Candlewick, 1995

Synopsis:

Little Nutbrown Hare asks Big Nutbrown Hare a simple question, "Guess How Much I Love You?" The result is a delightful procession of declarations of love, which they act out. The characters' genders remain unspecified, so that adults can personalize the relationship between the characters. An Abby Award Winner, this book is a grand display of unabashed, unconditional love.

Spiritual themes:

love, unconditional love, faithfulness, communication, companionship, joy, creativity, imagination, devotion

Scriptural application:

And may the Lord make you increase and abound in love for one another and for all, just as we abound in love for you.—1 Thessalonians 3:12

Spiritual reflection:

1. The Hares show more and more love for one another as the book progresses. Who does the Bible verse say will make us have greater and more obvious love for one another?

2. What do you think caused Little Nutbrown Hare to ask the question in the first place? Have you ever felt so much love for someone that you just had to tell them? Share your experience.

Activity:
Guess How Much I Love...

Encourage the children to think about someone that they love. Ask them to act out the ways in which they love this person, using the Hares' demonstration as inspiration.

THE HELLO, GOODBYE WINDOW

BY NORTON JUSTER
ILLUSTRATED BY CHRIS RASCHKA

New York: Michael Di Capua Books/Hyperion Books for Children, 2005

Synopsis:

A little girl tells the story of the kitchen window in her Nanny and Poppy's house. She calls it the "Hello, Goodbye Window" and explains it is not a regular window. The little girl describes the kitchen and the activities that take place there. The little girl explains how the window and what one can see through it is different at night. In the morning the window shows the little girl the weather and all the morning activities in the neighborhood. Some days, after a long day of playing outside, the little girl just sits by the window and waits for the unexpected to pass by. *The Hello, Goodbye Window* is always right where you need it.

Spiritual themes:

Family relationships, joys of "everyday" life, the wonders of imagination, living in community, joy of children

Scriptural application:

So teach us to count our days that we may gain a wise heart.
—Psalm 90:12

Activity:
Everyday Life Collage

Materials needed:

Pictures of children and families doing everyday things (eating, bike riding, walking the dog, etc.), construction paper, glue, markers, scissors.

Pass out construction paper to the children. Ask them to use the markers to draw a window on the construction paper. Lay out the pictures in front of them and ask them to find pictures of activities they see outside the windows in their house. Ask them to glue the pictures inside their windows.

Use this activity as an opportunity to talk with the children about how God is part of the everyday, ordinary things in our lives and that participating in the ordinary events of life can give us joy and happiness.

HOPE

BY ISABELL MONK
ILLUSTRATED BY JANICE LEE PORTER

Minneapolis: Carolrhoda, 1999

Synopsis:

School Library Journal calls this book "a must-have title." When Hope visits her Aunt Poogee for a weekend in the country, she hears enjoyable stories and meets colorful characters. Yet, a thoughtless comment about Hope's biracial features hurts Hope's feelings. Aunt Poogee explains that Hope's name reflects her parents' love for each other and faith in the future, and so does the blend of African American and Caucasian American traits that makes Hope unique. This book is a celebration of interethnic, interracial marriage and family, family history and traditions, intergenerational love, individuality, and resilience. Lush paintings and a delightful story make this an excellent resource for teaching children about race, faith, hope, and love.

Spiritual themes:

love, faith, hope, prayer, kindness, gentleness, multiculturalism, multiraciality, sharing, family love and heritage, intergenerational relationship, social justice, cultural survival, persistence, resilience, education, goals, hard work, civil rights, peace, treating others as we would want to be treated, family stories, appreciation for differences, the pain caused by judging and criticizing others, value of each unique person, humor, acceptance, hospitality

Scriptural application:

And now faith, hope, and love abide, these three;
and the greatest of these is love.—1 Corinthians 13:13

Spiritual reflection:

1. What does faith mean to you? hope? love?
2. How does your family story reflect faith? hope? love?
3. What parts of the book show Hope's family's faith?
4. What parts of the book show her family's hope?
5. What parts of the book show her family's love?

Activity:
Faith, Hope, and Love Family Tree

Materials needed:

green, brown, and other colors of construction paper, scissors, glue, markers/pens/crayons

Aunt Poogee's story shows that faith, hope, and love are a large part of Hope's family tree. What things are a part of your family tree? Have children cut a tree trunk out of brown paper and glue it to a piece of construction paper. Next, ask the children to cut out several leaves (5–7) from green paper. (To save time, teachers could have leaves and tree trunks prepared beforehand.) Ask the children to think about their own family tree and the family themes that it demonstrates. (Faith, hope, love, peace, multiraciality, multiethnicity, culture, humor, hard work, prayer, peace, sharing, mercy, togetherness, praise, worship, education, never giving up, and travel are examples of family themes.) Write one of these qualities on each leaf and glue the leaves onto the tree trunk. Finally, have the children write their names on the tree trunk as a celebration of the family traits that make them who they are.

IN GOD'S NAME

BY SANDY EISENBERG SASSO
ILLUSTRATED BY PHOEBE STONE

Woodstock, Vermont: Jewish Lights, 1994

Synopsis:

Lavish paintings depicting people of various ages, races, cultures, and occupations distinguish this Children's Books of Distinction Award Finalist. People pray, addressing God by the names that express their conception and relationship with God. When the people begin to judge and to criticize one another, their prayers are no longer heard. Only walking in love and tolerance opens the door to sharing and opens the ear of God.

Spiritual themes:

prayer, multiculturalism, multiraciality, tolerance, acceptance of others, love, parenting, family, giving, working, praise, worship, dedication to God, honoring God

Scriptural application:

O Lord, our Sovereign, how majestic is your name in all the earth!
—Psalm 8:9

Spiritual reflection:

1. What are some names for God in the Bible? What are some names for God that you have heard?

2. When the people were arguing, what happened? What happened when they showed respect for one another? When did God hear their prayers?

3. When do you pray? What name do you use for God?

Activity:
Names for God

Encourage children to think of Who God is to them. What names do they have for God? An adult may write these names down and share others from the Bible.

JOSEPH HAD A LITTLE OVERCOAT

WRITTEN AND ILLUSTRATED BY SIMMS TABACK

New York: Viking, 1999

Synopsis:

Joseph, a Jewish farmer, had an overcoat. When it wore out, he used creativity to make the remainder into a progression of useful items. A simple story about creativity, stewardship, recycling, village life, cultural celebration, and wisdom is enlivened by spectacular illustrations. Winner of the Caldecott Medal, this book features pictures made with gouache, watercolors, pen and ink, and collage. Creative illustrations combine social and cultural details to share insights into life in a Jewish village and culture.

Spiritual themes:

creativity, resourcefulness, stewardship, family life, contentment, persistence, overcoming adversity, cheerfulness, cultural heritage, family relationships, simplicity, rural life, resilience, thankfulness

Scriptural application:

I, wisdom, live with prudence, and I attain knowledge and discretion.
—Proverbs 8:12

Spiritual reflection:

1. When Joseph's overcoat is worn-out, what does he do? Instead of getting upset or disappointed, how does he use wisdom and creativity to solve his problems?

2. Have you ever felt like you had nothing? What did you do? How did you make something out of nothing?

Activity:
Sing!

This book is based on a Yiddish folk song called "I Had a Little Overcoat." This song appears at the end of the book. Sing this song once through. Then, sing it again and act it out as you go.

KITTEN'S FIRST FULL MOON

BY KEVIN HENKES

New York: Greenwillow Books, 2004

Synopsis:

A hungry kitten spots her first full moon and thinks it is a bowl of milk. She has many adventures chasing after it. She finds herself with bugs in her mouth, tumbling down the stairs, climbing a very tall tree and leaping into a pond. She goes back home and finds a bowl of milk waiting for her on the porch.

Spiritual themes:

Sometimes things are not always what they seem to be, Sometimes the things we really want and need are right in front of us but we don't see them until after we get into some trouble, Sometimes we need to let others take care of us, It is good and right to come home after we have left and gotten into some trouble.

Scriptural application:

Then Jesus said, "There was a man who had two sons. The younger of them said to his father, 'Father, give me the share of the property that will belong to me.' So he divided his property between them. A few days later the younger son gathered all he had and traveled to a distant country, and there he squandered his property in dissolute living. When he had spent everything, a severe famine took place throughout that country, and he began to be in need. So he went and hired himself out to one of the citizens of that country, who sent him to his fields to feed the pigs. He would gladly have filled himself with the pods that the pigs were eating; and no one gave him anything. But when he came to himself he said, 'How many of my father's hired hands have bread enough and to spare, but here I am dying of hunger! I will get up and go to my father, and I will say to him, "Father, I have sinned against heaven and before you; I am no longer worthy to be called your son; treat me like one of your hired hands."' So he set off and went to his father. But while he was still far off, his father saw him and was filled with compassion; he ran and put his arms around him and kissed him. Then the son said to him, 'Father, I have sinned against heaven and before you; I am no longer worthy to be called your son.' But the father said to his slaves, 'Quickly, bring out a robe—the best one—and put it on him; put a ring on his finger and sandals on his feet. And get the fatted calf and kill it, and let us eat and celebrate; for this son of mine was dead and is alive again; he was lost and is found!' And they began to celebrate.—Luke 15:11–24

Spiritual reflection:

1. Why did the kitten chase the moon and jump into the pond? What do you think the kitten thought about the bowl of milk when she went through all her difficulties (bugs, tumbling down the stairs, tall tree, falling in the pond)? Have you ever run after something you really wanted and found out it wasn't what you thought it would be?

2. What did the kitten find when she returned home? What do you think she thought about her adventure when she found the bowl of milk sitting on the porch?

Activity:
What Do You See?

Materials needed:

Various pictures of optical illusions. If you do an internet search for "optical illusions" you'll find many you can print.

Show the children the optical illusions. Talk about what they can see or can't see. Explain how sometimes things we see or want are not always what we think they are or will be. You can connect this to the kitten confusing the moon with a real bowl of milk or with the son not being content with what he had at home—wanting what he didn't have.

MAMA, DO YOU LOVE ME?

BY BARBARA M. JOOSSE
ILLUSTRATED BY BARBARA LAVALLEE

San Francisco: Chronicle, 1991

Synopsis:

Amid Arctic snow and wildlife, an Inuit mother and child express their unconditional love for one another. This genuine, delightful book can be used as an allegory of God's love. In addition to its touching story, a glossary at the end of the book educates readers about Native life in Alaska. Gorgeous watercolor paintings illustrate the life-ways, clothing, and animals that surround this family.

Spiritual themes:

love, unconditional love, parent-child relationships, discipline, understanding, communication, restoration, faithfulness, stability, imagination, creativity, forgiveness

Scriptural application:

The Lord appeared to him from far away.
I have loved you with an everlasting love;
therefore I have continued my faithfulness to you.—Jeremiah 31:3

Spiritual reflection:

1. In the story, the mother says that she will always love her child. The Bible calls God's love "everlasting." What does everlasting love mean to you?

2. If the child does something that the mother doesn't like or that is bad for the family, what does the mother say that she will do? Will she stop loving her child?

3. God loves you, all the time. How does that make you feel?

Activity:
Puppet Theatre

Materials needed:

colored construction paper, scissors, markers/crayons

Draw the characters from the story. Cut them out. Cut out a piece of paper and tape it to the back of each puppet, in order to make a ring that will fit on the child's finger. Make background scene. Slip the puppet over the child's fingers. With a puppet on each hand, act out the story.

OLIVER BUTTON IS A SISSY

STORY AND PICTURES BY TOMIE DEPAOLA

New York: Harcourt Brace Jovanovich, 1979

Synopsis:

Oliver Button would rather jump rope or walk in the woods than play football or other sports. He studies and attends dance classes, which cause his classmates to tease him unmercifully. The book's title is taken from a piece of graffiti that appears on the wall at Oliver's school. Yet, Oliver Button continues to practice. His gifts and talents for performing change his classmates' attitudes and the message on the wall.

Spiritual themes:

family love and relationships, acceptance of differences, treating others as we would want to be treated, gender roles and differences, performing arts, individuality, gifts and talents, persistence, the need for kindness, conquering fear, gentleness and self-control, love

Scriptural application:

Put away from you all bitterness and wrath and anger and wrangling and slander, together with all malice, and be kind to one another,

tenderhearted, forgiving one another, as God in Christ has forgiven you.
—Ephesians 4:31–32

Spiritual reflection:

1. Why did Oliver Button's classmates tease him? Why didn't his father understand him? How did they think a boy should act? How did Oliver Button act? Why was it wrong for them to treat him cruelly and make fun of him? How do you think that made him feel?

2. According to the Bible verse we just read, does God care about the way we treat other people? How does God treat us?

3. Oliver's classmates misunderstood and mistreated him. They even wrote a mean message on the schoolyard wall. How did they try to make up for hurting Oliver's feelings? How do you think that the new message made Oliver feel?

Activity:
Apology Letter

Materials needed:

paper, pens, or pencils

Have you ever teased anyone or hurt their feelings? How do you think that made them feel? The Bible tells us that when we hurt other people, we sin against God. Take a few minutes and write a letter to the person that you teased or mistreated, telling them that you are sorry and asking for their forgiveness. It doesn't matter if you can deliver the letter or if you even know or speak to this person. If children want to give the letter to the person, they may. Next, write a letter to someone who hurt your feelings. Let them know what they did that hurt your feelings and how their behavior made you feel. Forgive them, and tell them so in the letter. After that letter is finished, tear it up and throw it away. After all, when we confess and repent of our sins, God forgives us (Psalm 103). (If the children are too young to write, parents or teachers may write down what they say or encourage them to simply say what they would write in their letters.)

ON THE DAY YOU WERE BORN

WRITTEN AND ILLUSTRATED BY DEBRA FRASIER

San Diego: Harcourt Brace Jovanovich, 1991

Synopsis:

A colorful, festive celebration of the blessing of a new baby. This book is a hymn about the wonder of a new life joining the rhythms of creation, heralded by the animal kingdom, the astronomical realm, and rejoicing relatives and friends. As a special feature, the book offers readers an afterword, which discusses the species of animals illustrated and describes the actions of the earth, moon, and stars. Further, the author explains the patterns of the weather and tides and offers an introduction to the relationship between nature and the environment. Finally, Frasier introduces young readers to the meaning of population, individuality, and differences in skin color. As a result, *On the Day You Were Born* reinforces that each person is an individual and precious, while reminding readers of the importance of all life and of the environment.

Spiritual themes:

multiculturalism, each individual is a unique creation, family love and relationships, the majesty of God's creation, stewardship of the environment, diversity of God's creation, embracing differences, respect for all forms of life, interdependence between people and other life forms, the celebration of new life, and the joyous arrival of a new baby

Scriptural application:

I praise you, for I am fearfully and wonderfully made. Wonderful are your works; that I know very well.—Psalm 139:14

Spiritual reflection:

1. What do you like best about you? Least? According to Psalm 139:14, you are fearfully and wonderfully made. Take a minute and thank God for making you.

2. Throughout the book, we see many kinds of animals, insects, birds, and sea life. How would the world be different if any of these kinds of animals were missing (extinct)? What could we do to make sure that the earth is a good place to live for people and animals?

Activity:
String Paint a Celebration!

Materials needed:

string/twine (cut into pieces), tempera paint or other water-soluble paint, construction paper

Cover table and floors with newspaper and children with smocks. Provide each child with a piece of string or heavy twine. Pour a spoonful of paint into a corner of the piece of paper. Encourage children to paint the feelings of joy and celebration shared in this book by pulling string through the paint and across the paper, creating shapes, swirls, and designs.

THE PATCHWORK QUILT

BY VALERIE FLOURNOY
ILLUSTRATED BY JERRY PINKNEY

New York: Dial, 1985

Synopsis:

This Reading Rainbow and Coretta Scott King Award Winner for Nonviolent Social Change features a touching story and realistic watercolor paintings. When Tanya questions her grandmother about her collection of fabric scraps, Grandma tells Tanya that she plans to make a quilt. Tanya suggests that Grandma just buy one from the store. Grandma shares with Tanya that a handmade quilt will reflect the lives of this loving, African American family. The whole family becomes involved in helping to make Grandma's handcrafted quilt, which includes pieces of their clothing and their history. When Grandma falls ill and cannot work on the quilt, Tanya decides to continue the project. Her dedication and love for her grandmother earn Tanya a special reward—Grandma finishes the quilt and gives it to her!

Spiritual themes:

family love, respect for elders, cooperation, teamwork, respect for heritage and tradition, persistence, endurance, care and concern for others, sharing, generosity, love, kindness, goodness, helping others, giving, learning, wisdom, gentleness, cooperation between siblings, creation through arts and crafts, appreciation for handmade things (antimaterialism), and the value of unique creations and people

Scriptural application:

Let the favor of the Lord our God be upon us, and
prosper for us the work of our hands—
O prosper the work of our hands!—Psalm 90:17

Spiritual reflection:

1. This Bible verse is a prayer asking God to bless what we do. Have you ever asked God to help you to do something? Share your experience.

2. What is special about the quilt in this story? Why would Grandma want to make a quilt instead of buying one?

3. How does this quilt share the history and the story of Tanya's family? When Tanya is older, why do you think that this quilt will become even more special to her?

4. This quilt is the work of Grandma's hands, Tanya's hands, and a celebration of the whole family working together. What does this story teach us about how families show love for one another? How does love cause the work of their hands to prosper?

Activity:
Our Own Quilt

Materials needed

fabric squares (various sizes and colors), glue, scissors, construction paper

Cut fabric into squares of various colors and sizes. Allow children to select some squares. Then, have them glue the squares onto the construction paper to make a larger square—their own patchwork quilt.

PEOPLE

WRITTEN AND ILLUSTRATED BY PETER SPIER

Garden City, New York: Doubleday, 1980

Synopsis:

There are billions of people on the Earth. Each one is an individual, with specific culture, recreation, physical traits, and ethnicity. An outstanding introduction to diversity, *People* features intricate artwork that explores the distinctions between color, occupations, standards of beauty, religious beliefs, recreational activities, language, and other qualities. In this book, children learn that if people were all alike, the world would not be a rich and varied place. This book is an excellent way to teach multiculturalism, acceptance of others, diversity, and to begin to dismantle the components of prejudice.

Spiritual themes:

diversity of God's creation, multiculturalism, acceptance of others, friendship, tolerance, social justice, do not judge or criticize, peace, family life, each person is a precious and unique creation of God, sharing, learning, communication, understanding others, wisdom, kindness, love for other people and for ourselves

Scriptural application:

He said to him, 'You shall love the Lord your God with all your heart, and with all your soul, and with all your mind.' This is the greatest and first commandment. And a second is like it: 'You shall love your neighbor as yourself.'—Matthew 22:37–39

For this is the message you have heard from the beginning, that we should love one another.—1 John 3:11

Spiritual reflection:

1. Why do you think that God made so many different kinds of people? How many people do you know that are different from you in any way?

2. Do you like to meet or to know people that are different from you? Why or why not? How does God want us to treat people who are different from us?

3. Sometimes people think that people who are different from them are strange. Was there any person in the book that seemed strange to you? How might a person from one of the cultures in the book think that YOU are strange?

Activity:
A Celebration of People!

Materials needed:

markers/crayons, paper

After reading the book, ask children to draw as many kinds of people as they can think of in a specific amount of time allotted. No two people can be alike. Each one should be different in some way (age, occupations, physical ability, economics, appearance, activity, etc.). At the end of the allotted time, ask the children to count how many different people they drew. Remind them that God loves each person, and that Christians are commanded to love other people as well.

PETER'S CHAIR

BY EZRA JACK KEATS

New York: Viking, 1998

Synopsis:

It's bad enough that there's a new baby in Peter's family. Having a new baby sister means that Peter has to play quietly and doesn't get as much attention as he used to enjoy. Now, Peter's parents expect him to give up his furniture! Enough is enough! Faced with the prospect of watching his blue furniture become pink, Peter seizes his chair and runs away. He only gets as far as the front porch, but the process allows him to consider what it means to be the big brother and to share. Dazzling artwork, and a welcome portrayal of a solid African American family make this a great book for children with younger siblings or for families to read together.

Spiritual themes:

love, family love, sharing, sibling love, generosity, working together, helping others, making sacrifices, selflessness, accepting change, family growth, unity, agreement, processing anger

Scriptural application:

For God did not give us a spirit of cowardice, but rather a spirit of power and of love and of self-discipline.—2 Timothy 1:7

Spiritual reflection:

1. Why does Peter dislike the new baby? What are his reasons? How did fear cause him to act the way that he did?
2. Is there or has there ever been a new baby in your house? What did you like about having a new baby? What didn't you like?
3. Why does Peter take his chair and run away? What makes him change his mind? How do you think that he will treat his little sister from now on?

Activity:
Be a Cheerful Giver!

Materials needed:

paper, crayons/markers

Ask the children to think of something that they have that they could give away. Remind them that we are supposed to give good things, not trash or worn-out things. Make a gift tag for the item that they plan to give away.

THE RUNAWAY BUNNY

BY MARGARET WISE BROWN
PICTURES BY CLEMENT HURD

New York and London: Harper, 1942

Synopsis:

A bunny repeatedly questions his mother concerning the depths of her love.

Spiritual themes:

love, parent-child bonds, faithfulness, God's love, forgiveness, unconditional love, boundaries and limits, obedience, patience, gentleness, goodness, mercy, persistence, an allegory for God's salvation

Scriptural application:

Which one of you, having a hundred sheep and losing one of them, does not leave the ninety-nine in the wilderness and go after the one that is lost until he finds it? When he has found it, he lays it on his shoulders and rejoices. And when he comes home, he calls together his friends and neighbors, saying to them, "Rejoice with me, for I have found my sheep that was lost." Just so, I tell you, there will be more joy in heaven over one sinner who repents than over ninety-nine righteous persons who need no repentance.—Luke 15:4–7

Spiritual reflection:

1. Why would the bunny want to run away? What does the mother bunny say about this idea? What would she do to find her little bunny?

2. Compare this story to the Bible verses that we read. When the shepherd lost one sheep, what did he do? Since he had 99 others, why do you think that one sheep meant so much to him?

3. God loves each person very much. How does this book show us something about God's love for us? How do we see God's love in the Bible verses we read?

Activity:
Bring Bunny Home

Materials needed:

A picture of a bunny (cut out), or a small stuffed bunny

Prior to reading the story, hide the bunny. Provide the children with a clue to finding the bunny. Prepare to provide additional clues, if needed. Encourage children to work together to find the bunny and bring it "home." If time permits, hide the bunny again or allow children to take turns hiding the bunny.

THE SNOWY DAY

BY EZRA JACK KEATS

New York: Puffin, 1976

Synopsis:

Lavish illustrations celebrate the majesty of a snowfall. This Caldecott Medal winner invites readers to go outside and play with a young African American boy. Making tracks in the snow, building a snowman, and making a snowball are all part of the wonders of a snowy day. This book provides an excellent opportunity to explain the changing of the seasons to children, to explore the beauty of God's creation, and to discover the spiritual value of play.

Spiritual themes:

God's creation, seasons and nature, recreation and play, family love, imagination, creativity, discovery, friendship, wonder, appreciation for beauty

Scriptural application:

Happy are the people to whom such blessings fall; happy are the people whose God is the Lord.—Psalm 144:15

Spiritual reflection:

1. Have you ever had a pleasant surprise? How was the snow a treat for the boy?
2. Think about the best day you can remember. What happened to make it so special?
3. Just when the boy thinks that the snow is melted forever, what happens? Have you ever expected something to go wrong that turned out right instead? How did you feel then?

Activity:
Your Own Snowy Day!

Materials needed:

clean baby food (or other clear) jars with lids, white or silver glitter/snowflake-shaped glitter, glue, water, small plastic people/animals/buildings/etc.

Glue plastic objects inside of the jar lid. Allow glue to dry thoroughly. Next, place approximately a tablespoon of glitter in the bottom of the baby food jar. Fill the jar with tap water. Put the lid on the jar and make sure that it is secure. Gently shake the jar to see the glitter snowfall!

SOMETHING SPECIAL FOR ME

BY VERA B. WILLIAMS

New York: Greenwillow, 1983

Synopsis:

Rosa, Grandma, and Mama have been saving their money for awhile. They decide that Rosa should celebrate her birthday by using their savings to buy a gift for herself. As Rosa considers what she should buy, she hears an accordion player. Rosa makes the choice to buy a present for everyone! A portrayal of a loving Hispanic family, this American Library Association Notable Book uses bright, colorful watercolor paintings and detailed borders to tell the story of a special gift and a delightful giver.

Spiritual themes:

generosity, giving, sharing, love, family love, intergenerational bonds, music, persistence, overcoming economic limitations, selflessness, concern for others, saving, setting goals, problem solving, creativity

Scriptural application:

Love one another with mutual affection; outdo one another in showing honor.—Romans 12:10

Spiritual reflection:

1. How did the family show concern for Rosa above themselves? How did Rosa show concern for others beside herself?

2. Why is Rosa's gift special? What would have happened if she had kept the coins for herself or bought something for herself only?

Activity:
Personal Symphony

Materials needed:

glass drinking glasses, water, teaspoons

In the story, Rosa gave the gift of music to her family. Why not compose your own music? Fill drinking glasses with different amounts of tap water. Because of the different water levels, each glass will make a different tone when tapped. GENTLY tap the teaspoon on the side of the glasses to create your own music!

THE STORY OF RUBY BRIDGES

BY ROBERT COLES
ILLUSTRATED BY GEORGE FORD

New York: Scholastic, 1995

Synopsis:

In 1960, Ruby Bridges integrated an all-Caucasian elementary school in New Orleans. Caucasian parents and community members persecuted this African American child relentlessly. Each day, Ruby Bridges endured a walk past cursing adults, federal marshals as escorts, and the isolation of learning in a classroom separated from the other students. The book, illustrated with moving paintings, shows the source of Ruby's resilience—her prayers and her family's faith.

Spiritual themes:

faith, prayer, loving your enemies, forgiveness, persecution, prejudice, multiculturalism, diversity, loneliness, education, hope, love, family love, ending racism and prejudice, repentance, grief, sorrow, dealing with insults and hurt, mercy, the dangers of judging and criticism, overcoming fear

Scriptural application:

Do not judge, and you will not be judged:
do not condemn, and you will not be condemned.
Forgive, and you will be forgiven.—Luke 6:37

But I say to you, love your enemies and pray
for those who persecute you.—Matthew 5:44

Spiritual reflection:

1. The parents in the story abused Ruby Bridges because she was African American. They didn't take the time to find out the kind of person Ruby was. The scripture that we read calls that kind of behavior judging and condemning. What happens when we judge and condemn other people?

2. If parents had known what Ruby was really like, do you think that they would have changed their behavior? How?

3. Even though she was mistreated through no fault of her own, Ruby Bridges prayed for her enemies. How did that show the love of God toward them? How does that obey what the Bible says to do?

Activity:
Intercessory Prayer

The Bible tells us to pray for our enemies. Do you have any enemies? Is there anyone who hurt you or who is hurting you right now? Take a moment to think about how Ruby Bridges acted when she was being mistreated. Now, pray and forgive the people that have hurt you. Then, consider anyone that you have teased, abused, judged, or condemned. Pray for that person and ask God to forgive you for how you have behaved. In groups, allow the children to form prayer partners, by placing them in pairs.

STRANGER IN THE WOODS:
A PHOTOGRAPHIC FANTASY

BY CARL R. SAMS II AND JEAN STOICK

Milford, Michigan: Carl R. Sams II Photography, 2000

Synopsis:

Two children build a special "stranger in the woods." Their snowman provides a carrot and corn for the deer, nuts and seeds for the birds, and excitement for all of the creatures in the woods. A Benjamin Franklin Award winner, this book features outstanding photographs, which illustrate the richness of life in the woods. The message of the book teaches children to respect the environment and all of God's creatures.

Spiritual themes:

giving, sharing, sibling cooperation and friendship, stewardship of God's creation, environmental awareness, God's creation, diversity of life, beauty of nature

Scriptural application:

You make springs gush forth in the valleys;

they flow between the hills,

giving drink to every wild animal;

the wild asses quench their thirst.

By the streams the birds of the air have their habitation;

they sing among the branches.

From your lofty abode you water the mountains;

the earth is satisfied with the fruit of your work.

You cause the grass to grow for the cattle,

and plants for people to use,

to bring forth food from the earth,

and wine to gladden the human heart,

oil to make the face shine,

and bread to strengthen the human heart.

The trees of the Lord are watered abundantly,

the cedars of Lebanon that he planted.

In them the birds build their nests;

the stork has its home in the fir trees.

The high mountains are for the wild goats;

the rocks are a refuge for the coneys.

—Psalm 104:10–18

Spiritual reflection:

1. Name some of the things that God made that appear in Psalm 104.

2. What did the animals think when they found out that there was a "stranger" in their woods? Why were some of the animals afraid? Why are strangers dangerous to many animals?

3. Why did the animals decide that the stranger was "friendly"? What made them glad to see this "stranger"?

4. How did the children work together to help the animals? How did their snowman show that they cared about the creatures in the forest?

5. What can you do to show you care about nature, the environment, and the life forms around you?

Activity:
Build a Snowman!

The final pages of the book feature a "recipe for a snowman" that provides winter fun for children and snacks for animals. Head outside and build a snowman. In the absence of real snow, ask the children to act out the parts of the animals, the snowman, and the children as an adult or another child reads the story out loud.

THIS IS NOT MY HAT

BY JON KLASSEN

Somerville, MA: Candlewick Press, 2012

Synopsis:

A small fish steals a hat from a big fish while the big fish is asleep. The little fish is convinced the big fish won't notice the hat is missing. And the little fish believes that even if he does notice it missing the big fish won't know who took it. And even if he does figure out it is the little fish, the big fish won't know where the little fish is. The little fish does tell the reader he is going to where the plants are big and tall and grow together. It is a place where no one will ever find him. A crab spies the little fish but promises not to tell anyone which way he went. But the crab does tell the big fish where the little fish went. The little fish confesses that he knows it is wrong to steal the hat but since the hat is too small for the big fish he is going to keep it anyway. The big fish finds the little fish and takes his hat back.

Spiritual themes:

Stealing from others is wrong, it is easy to make our wrongdoing seem right, choosing to do the right thing

Scriptural applications:

You shall not steal.—Exodus 20:15

Anyone, then, who knows the right thing to do and fails to do it, commits sin.—James 4:17

Spiritual reflection

1. Why do you think the little fish stole the hat? Why did the little fish think it was OK to steal the hat? Have you ever done something wrong and then convinced yourself that it was the right thing to do? Why do you think God says it is wrong to steal?
2. Let's talk about the crab. He told the little fish he wouldn't tell on him and then he told the big fish where he was. What do you think the crab did that was right? Why do you think it was right? Do you think the crab did anything wrong? Why do you think it was wrong?

Activity:
Crab and Fish Hand Paintings

Materials needed:

red, blue, and green washable paint, painting paper, paper towel/moist towelettes, markers, paper plates, large wiggle eyes, glue

Use one plate per paint color—pouring the paint on the plate. Set the plates in the middle of the table. Give each child a piece of paper. Instruct children to make a "crab" with their hands. (Press their wrists together and spread out fingers in such a way that each child can put the palms and fingers of both hands in the paint.) Use the red paint for this. After they lift their hands out of the paint have them press the "painted" part of their hands on the paper (still in the same configuration). This will make the body of the crab. Have children use a wet paper towel or moist towelettes to clean the red paint off their hands. Next have them print a "fish" by pressing all the fingers of their hand together with the thumb sticking up like a fin. Have the children press down their palms, fingers, and thumbs into the blue or green paint and then print the "fish" on the paper. Provide a wet paper towel or moist towelettes to clean the paint off everyone's hands. Give each child two large wiggle eyes and some glue. Instruct them to glue the eyes on the top of their thumb prints on the crab. Ask them to color in the rest of the "seascape" using the markers.

As they print their "crab" and "fish" talk about the characters in the story and each of their actions. Ask who acted in a good way and who did not.

THIS LAND IS YOUR LAND

BY WOODY GUTHRIE
ILLUSTRATED BY KATHY JAKOBSEN

Boston: Little, Brown, 1998

Synopsis:

Detailed oil paintings and an uncanny accuracy for details make this book a fascinating piece of biographical art. Folk musician Woody Guthrie's 1940s song is the text for the book, which is social commentary as well as a celebration of the people and landscapes of the United States.

Spiritual themes:

the beauty and majesty of God's creation, equality of people, acceptance of others, compassion for the poor and disenfranchised, liberty, freedom, diversity, multiculturalism, geographic/regional diversity and value, economic justice, social justice, performing arts, persistence, progress, inclusiveness, urban renewal, community empowerment, cooperation, family love, communication, sharing, giving, personal responsibility, work, music, joy, overcoming hardships, friendship, history, tradition, heritage, patriotism, social commentary, social action, charity, culture

Scriptural application:

If my people who are called by my name humble themselves, pray, seek my face, and turn from their wicked ways, then I will hear from heaven, and will forgive their sin and heal their land. —2 Chronicles 7:14

Spiritual reflection:

1. Woody Guthrie's song celebrates his travels throughout the United States. What did he see that was good? What did he see that needed to be changed?
2. How did people in the book work together to improve the places where they lived? How could you improve the place where you live?
3. In 2 Chronicles 7:14, Christians are commanded to pray for the country in which we live. What could we thank God for giving our nation? How could we ask God to help our nation?

Activity:
Take a Trip!

Materials needed:

A roadmap of the United States (or country where children reside), self-adhesive stars or stickers, markers

Ask the children to name every state that they have visited. In a family, each member should name the places that they have visited. Mark these with stars. If time permits, they may name individual cities and towns. Connect these stars or stickers with a marker to show the personal journey of the group, family, or individual child. Next, pray for the country. Then, sing "This Land is Your Land," found at the close of the book.

THE VELVETEEN RABBIT

BY MARGERY WILLIAMS

(Various editions)

Synopsis:

A classic tale of a young boy's love for his stuffed rabbit, whose great desire is to be "real." The rabbit accompanies the boy throughout his life. When the child falls ill with fever, his stuffed bunny is his constant companion. After the boy's illness, all of the things he touched during his confinement must be destroyed. The rabbit is no longer allowed to be near his friend, but is rewarded for his faithfulness by becoming "real." As described by Williams, reality and significance are a result of loving and being loved.

Spiritual themes:

love, generosity, selflessness, sacrifice, faithfulness, loyalty, loss, grief, healing, friendship, meaning and significance, kindness, trust

Scriptural application:

A friend loves at all times, and kinsfolk are born to share adversity.
—Proverbs 17:17

Spiritual reflection:

1. This Bible verse tells us that friends should be loyal to one another, showing love even in hard times. How do you show love for your friends? How did the rabbit show his love for the child?

2. What did the rabbit do when the child became sick? How did he show love for his friend in a difficult time?

3. Have you ever shown love to someone in your life when they were having a hard time? Share about it. Has someone ever shown love for you when you were going through difficulties?

4. Staying with the boy during sickness seemed to cost the rabbit everything at first, but something good came out of it. What happened?

Activity:
Pantomime

After reading the story, encourage children to act it out silently. In groups, allow each child to portray a character. With fewer children, encourage them to act it out in their own way—only without words.

WHAT'S WRONG WITH TIMMY?

BY MARIA SHRIVER
ILLUSTRATED BY SANDRA SPEIDEL

Boston: Little, Brown, 2001

Synopsis:

A sensitive and generous story about what happens when Timmy, a child with a disability, looks and acts differently. Ms. Shriver tells a beautiful story that helps parents and children talk about differences while embracing the things that people have in common.

Spiritual themes:

love for neighbor, support and friendship, ministry of children to teach, appreciation of differences, sharing, giving, inclusion, courage, strength from difficulty, and encouragement

Scriptural application:

We have gifts that differ according to the grace given to us: prophecy, in proportion to faith; ministry, in ministering; the teacher, in teaching; the exhorter, in exhortation; the giver, in generosity; the leader, in diligence;

the compassionate, in cheerfulness. . . . Rejoice with those who rejoice, weep with those who weep.—Romans 12:6–8, 15

Spiritual reflection:

1. In the story, Kate talks with her mother when she realizes that she has questions about Timmy. Who do you talk with when you meet a child or adult who seems different and you have questions that you need to ask someone about those things that seem different to you? (Examples—a parent, grandparent, teacher, etc.)

2. In the story, Grandma explained to Kate that, "God makes all different types of children." Why and how is someone you know different from you? We must also remember that, while we may be different from one another, we have many things in common. How and why is this same person you named as different, just like you in many ways? (Examples—laughs, loves to read and learn about things, cares about others, goes to school, loves their family, wants friends, etc.)

3. "Each of us is here on earth for a reason and has a mission," says Kate's mom. God has given each person different gifts and talents to contribute to the world. Through their different gifts and talents, both Timmy and Kate helped other children learn about "being strong inside," to be more understanding, to be kind, to appreciate each person's gifts and talents, including others, and being friends. What did Kate do when she saw that other children were leaving Timmy out of their games and their circle of friends? What can you do when you see someone being excluded or treated unkindly because they seem different from others?

4. God loves each of us just the way we are. How does it make you feel to know that God loves you just the way you are?

Activity:
Collages

Materials needed:

drawing paper, colored tissue paper, fabric scraps of all kinds, glitter, crayons, colored construction paper, glue, tape, string and yarn strips, blunt scissors, assorted magazine pictures, a variety of other materials that can be glued to the drawing paper

Encourage the children to have fun making a collage that expresses their personalities. Allow them to tear, cut, rip, etc. the provided materials in order to glue them to the drawing paper in any pattern or way that they prefer. When everyone has completed their collage, invite each child to tell about their collage. Then in a group conversation, talk about how each one is similar to the others. Examples—colors used, glitter used, etc.

WHEN I WAS YOUNG IN THE MOUNTAINS

BY CYNTHIA RYLANT
ILLUSTRATED BY DIANE GOODE

New York: Dutton, 1982

Synopsis:

A woman recalls her childhood in Appalachia. This Caldecott Honor Book is a touching tale of a girl and her sister, who live with their grandparents in the mountains. Church attendance and baptism appear in a favorable light. Although the family's poverty is evident, the tale transcends economic limitations to show a loving family and a childhood filled with love and fun.

Spiritual themes:

family love, love, resourcefulness, courage, resilience, persistence, contentment, hard work, church attendance, salvation, baptism, community bonds, peace, nature, Christian faith, cooperation, sibling friendships, rural life, overcoming hardships, acceptance, trust, cheerfulness

Scriptural application:

Of course, there is great gain in godliness combined with contentment.
—1 Timothy 6:6

Spiritual reflection:

1. What does it mean to be content? The girl in the story says "I never wanted to go anywhere else in the world, for I was in the mountains. And that was always enough." How does this show contentment?

2. What does the girl like about her life in the mountains? What do you like about where you live?

Activity:
Using What You Have

Materials needed:

glue, cardboard squares, an assortment of objects (buttons, fabric, paper clips, magazine pictures, beads, string, etc.)

In the story, the people use what is available to them. The school is also the church, and the swimming hole is for playing as well as baptisms. Hand each child an assortment of items. Ask them to make a collage using what they have (no trading or exchanges) in front of them. Encourage them to be resourceful and to use creativity.

APPENDIX 1

THE FOLLOWING PRAYER, OR ONE OF YOUR OWN CHOOSING, MAY BE SHARED AT THE BEGINNING OF EACH SESSION:

We thank you God for this day and our time together. We are thankful for stories of everyday things that help us to see your love, care, and protection at work in our lives and in the lives of others. In Jesus' name, we pray. Amen.

A SUGGESTED CLOSING PRAYER:

Creator of the world

Help us love one another,

Help us care for each other

As sister and brother,

That friendship may grow

from house to house, from

neighborhood to neighborhood,

city to city, nation to nation.

Bring peace to our hearts and to our world

O wonderful Creator of us all.

APPENDIX II

SCRIPTURE REFERENCES FOR EACH SESSION:

I lie down and sleep; I wake again, for the Lord sustains me.—Psalm 3:5

I will both lie down and sleep in peace; for you alone, O Lord, make me lie down in safety.—Psalm 4:8

Which one of you, having a hundred sheep and losing one of them, does not leave the ninety-nine in the wilderness and go after the one that is lost until he finds it? When he has found it, he lays it on his shoulders and rejoices. And when he comes home, he calls together his friends and neighbors, saying to them, "Rejoice with me, for I have found my sheep that was lost." Just so, I tell you, there will be more joy in heaven over one sinner who repents than over ninety-nine righteous persons who need no repentance.—Luke 15:4–7

The earth is the Lord's and all that is in it, the world, and those who live in it.—Psalm 24:1

Do not judge, and you will not be judged; do not condemn, and you will not be condemned. Forgive, and you will be forgiven.—Luke 6:37

But I say to you, Love your enemies and pray for those who persecute you.—Matthew 5:44

Put away from you all bitterness and wrath and anger and wrangling and slander, together with all malice, and be kind to one another,

tenderhearted, forgiving one another, as God in Christ has forgiven you.
—Ephesians 4:31–32

Let the favor of the Lord our God be upon us, and prosper for us the work of our hands—O prosper the work of our hands!—Psalm 90:17

I praise you, for I am fearfully and wonderfully made. Wonderful are your works; that I know very well.—Psalm 139:14

If my people who are called by my name humble themselves, pray, seek my face, and turn from their wicked ways, then I will hear from heaven, and will forgive their sin and heal their land.—2 Chronicles 7:14

The Lord appeared to him from far away. I have loved you with an everlasting love; therefore I have continued my faithfulness to you.
—Jeremiah 31:3

For God did not give us a spirit of cowardice, but rather a spirit of power and of love and of self-discipline.—2 Timothy 1:7

Happy are the people to whom such blessings fall; happy are the people whose God is the Lord.—Psalm 144:15

And may the Lord make you increase and abound in love for one another and for all, just as we abound in love for you.—1 Thessalonians 3:12

And now faith, hope, and love abide, these three; and the greatest of these is love.—1 Corinthians 13:13

Children, obey your parents in the Lord, for this is right.—Ephesians 6:1

Now the Lord is the Spirit, and where the Spirit of the Lord is, there is freedom.—2 Corinthians 3:17

Of course, there is great gain in godliness combined with contentment.
—1 Timothy 6:6

Bless the Lord, O my soul.
O Lord my God, you are very great.
You are clothed with honor and majesty,
wrapped in light as with a garment.
You stretch out the heavens like a tent,
you set the beams of your chambers on the waters,
you make the clouds your chariot,
you ride on the wings of the wind,
you make the winds your messengers,
fire and flame your ministers.
You set the earth on its foundations,
so that it shall never be shaken.
You cover it with the deep as with a garment;
the waters stood above the mountains.
At your rebuke they flee;
at the sound of your thunder they take to flight.
They rose up to the mountains, ran down to the valleys
to the place that you appointed for them.
You set a boundary that they may not pass,
so that they might not again cover the earth.
You make springs gush forth in the valleys;
they flow between the hills,
giving drink to every wild animal;
the wild asses quench their thirst.
By the streams the birds of the air have their habitation;
they sing among the branches.
From your lofty abode you water the mountains;
the earth is satisfied with the fruit of your work.
You cause the grass to grow for the cattle,
and plants for people to use,
to bring forth food from the earth,
and wine to gladden the human heart,
oil to make the face shine,
and bread to strengthen the human heart.

The trees of the Lord are watered abundantly,
the cedars of Lebanon that he planted.
In them the birds build their nests;
the stork has its home in the fir trees.
The high mountains are for the wild goats;
the rocks are a refuge for the coneys.
You have made the moon to mark the seasons;
the sun knows its time for setting.
You make darkness, and it is night,
when all the animals of the forest come creeping out.
The young lions roar for their prey,
seeking their food from God.
When the sun rises, they withdraw
and lie down in their dens.
People go out to their work
and to their labor until the evening.
O Lord, how manifold are your works!
In wisdom you have made them all;
the earth is full of your creatures.
Yonder is the sea, great and wide,
creeping things innumerable are there,
living things both small and great.
There go the ships,
and Leviathan that you formed to sport in it.
These all look to you
to give them their food in due season;
when you give to them, they gather it up;
when you open your hand, they are filled with good things.
When you hide your face, they are dismayed;
when you take away their breath, they die
and return to their dust.
When you send forth your spirit, they are created;
and you renew the face of the ground.
May the glory of the Lord endure forever;
may the Lord rejoice in his works—
who looks on the earth and it trembles,

who touches the mountains and they smoke.
I will sing to the Lord as long as I live;
I will sing praise to my God while I have being.
May my meditation be pleasing to him,
for I rejoice in the Lord.
Let sinners be consumed from the earth,
and let the wicked be no more.
Bless the Lord, O my soul.
Praise the Lord!—Psalm 104

Now when Jesus came into the district of Caesarea Philippi, he asked his disciples, 'Who do people say that the Son of Man is?' And they said, 'Some say John the Baptist, but others Elijah, and still others Jeremiah or one of the prophets.' He said to them, 'But who do you say that I am?' Simon Peter answered, 'You are the Messiah, the Son of the living God.' And Jesus answered him, 'Blessed are you, Simon son of Jonah! For flesh and blood has not revealed this to you, but my [Parent] in heaven.'
—Matthew 16:13–17

O Lord, our Sovereign, how majestic is your name in all the earth!
—Psalm 8:9

We have gifts that differ according to the grace given to us: prophecy, in proportion to faith; ministry, in ministering; the teacher, in teaching; the exhorter, in exhortation; the giver, in generosity; the leader, in diligence; the compassionate, in cheerfulness. . . . Rejoice with those who rejoice, weep with those who weep.—Romans 12:6–8, 15

He said to him, 'You shall love the Lord your God with all your heart, and with all your soul, and with all your mind.' This is the greatest and first commandment. And a second is like it: 'You shall love your neighbor as yourself.'—Matthew 22:37–39

For this is the message you have heard from the beginning, that we should love one another.—1 John 3:11

Love never ends.—1 Corinthians 13:8

I, wisdom, live with prudence, and I attain knowledge and discretion.
—Proverbs 8:12

A friend loves at all times, and kinsfolk are born to share adversity.
—Proverbs 17:17

Love one another with mutual affection; outdo one another in showing honor.—Romans 12:10

Pray without ceasing.—1 Thessalonians 5:17

He answered, 'You shall love the Lord your God with all your heart, and with all your soul, and with all your strength, and with all your mind; and your neighbor as yourself.' And he said to him, 'You have given the right answer; do this, and you will live.' But wanting to justify himself, he asked Jesus, 'And who is my neighbor?' Jesus replied, 'A man was going down from Jerusalem to Jericho, and fell into the hands of robbers, who stripped him, beat him, and went away, leaving him half dead. Now by chance a priest was going down that road; and when he saw him, he passed by on the other side. So likewise a Levite, when he came to the place and saw him, passed by on the other side. But a Samaritan while traveling came near him; and when he saw him, he was moved with pity. He went to him and bandaged his wounds, having poured oil and wine on them. Then he put him on his own animal, brought him to an inn, and took care of him. The next day he took out two denarii, gave them to the innkeeper, and said, 'Take care of him; and when I come back, I will repay you whatever more you spend.' Which of these three, do you think, was a neighbor to the man who fell into the hands of the robbers?' He said, 'The one who showed him mercy.' Jesus said to him, 'Go and do likewise.'
—Luke 10:27–37

Bear one another's burdens, and in this way you will fulfill the law of Christ.—Galatians 6:2

APPENDIX III

ADDITIONAL BOOKS FOR READING:

To Be a Kid

BY MAYA AJMERA AND JOHN D. IVANKO

Watertown, Massachusetts: Charlesbridge, 1999

El Conejito Andarin (Runaway Bunny)

BY MARGARET WISE BROWN

ILLUSTRATED BY CLEMENT HURD

New York: HarperCollins, 1995

The Bat Boy & His Violin

BY GAVIN CURTIS

ILLUSTRATED BY E.B. LEWIS

New York: Simon & Schuster, 1998

The Night of Las Posadas
WRITTEN AND ILLUSTRATED BY TOMIE DEPAOLA

New York: Putnam, 1999

I'm Your Child, God: Prayers for Children and Teenagers
BY MARIAN WRIGHT EDELMAN

ILLUSTRATED BY BRYAN COLLIER

New York: Hyperion, 2002

Adoption is for Always
BY LINDA WALVOORD GIRARD

ILLUSTRATED BY JUDITH FRIEDMAN

Morton Grove, Illinois: Albert Whitman, 1986

La Pesca De Nessa (Nessa's Fish)
BY NANCY LUENN

ILLUSTRATED BY NEIL WALDMAN

TRANSLATION BY ALMA FLOR ADA

New York: Macmillian International, 1994

Nessa's Story
BY NANCY LUENN

ILLUSTRATED BY NEIL WALDMAN

New York: Macmillian International, 1994

Blanca's Feather
BY ANTONIO HERNÁNDEZ MADRIGAL

ILLUSTRATED BY SUZAN GERARDO

Flagstaff, Arizona: Rising Moon, 2000

Somewhere Today: A Book of Peace
BY SHELLEY MOORE THOMAS

PHOTOGRAPHS BY ERIC FUTRAN

Morton Grove, Illinois: Albert Whitman, 1998